Microcosm Publishing is Portland's most diversified publishing house and distributor with a focus on the colorful, authentic, and empowering. Our books and zines have put your power in your hands since 1996, equipping readers to make positive changes in their lives and in the world around them. Microcosm emphasizes skill-building, showing hidden histories, and fostering creativity through challenging conventional publishing wisdom with books and bookettes about DIY skills, food, bicycling, gender, self-care, and social justice. What was once a distro and record label was started by Joe Biel in his bedroom and has become among the oldest independent publishing houses in Portland, OR. We are a politically moderate, centrist publisher in a world that has inched to the right for the past 80 years.

Introduction

Thank you for picking up a copy of *This Zine Has Issues #3: Bipolar Disorder*. In the following pages you'll find poetry, a book review, essays, and art by many contributors, all for the purpose of breaking stigma and helping those of us who experience bipolar disorder know that we are not alone. Having said that, it's important to note that much of the content comes with a general warning for triggers such as anxiety, suicidal ideation, trauma, depression, PTSD, mania, abuse, and other things related to mental illnesses. So please, proceed with caution.

Why David on the cover?

The subject of Michelangelo's sculpture, ancient Israel's King David, was a shepherd, musician, psalmist, slayer of Goliath the giant Philistine, adulterer, murderer of Bathsheba's husband Uriah the Hittite, ancestor of Jesus of Nazareth, and described by the Hebrew scriptures as, "a man after God's own heart." King David is also believed by some to have been bipolar. (Take a look at David's extreme moods in his Psalms.) I have bipolar disorder and happen to be named after the same David, so that's why I chose him for the cover.

I'd like to take a moment to thank all of the talented contributors for sharing their work with the readers of This Zine. Also, a special thank you to Jen Aboki for feedback about the previous issues and for sharing her thoughts about the cover. Her illustration "I Am Not Your Labels" is featured on page 31 and her stickersheet design is shown on page 30.

If you'd like to send your feedback about This Zine, please drop me a line at: *thiszinehasissues@gmail.com*. I'd love to hear from you about what was good, bad, beautiful, informative, etc. about the issue. I'll be printing emails in the zine from readers going forward, so please, write and share your thoughts. By the way, what should we name the new letters column? Suggestions welcome!

Also of note, please check out our shiny new website at *thiszinehasissues.com*. It's a work in progress, but so far we've got an online shop (with stickers), a blog, links to stores where you can purchase *This Zine* and more stuff on the way.

This Zine is coming to a major crossroads and there are big changes in store starting with issue 4. Hang with us as there may be a longer gap between issues while we implement the changes. Having said all that, thanks for reading and I hope you'll enjoy the issue!

– Dave Combs

Next Up - *TZHI #4: Music and Mental Health* or *The Arts and Mental Health* ...help us decide!

This Zine Has Issues #3: Bipolar Disorder

Contributors

Tiffany Woods
Stetson University Class of 2015

Mike Vinopal
IG: @mikevinopal

Crystal Raypole
Twitter: @CrystalRaypole

emjivi
IG/Twitter: @emjivi

Andrew Diaz
artbyandrewdiaz.com

Dorota Chioma
IG: @dorota.chioma.art

Dave Combs
IG: @davemakesstickers

Holly Combs
IG: @hollycombs_

Shades
shadesdraws.tumblr.com

Ruth River
IG: @call.me.river

Nikki Reed
IG: @spastic.sanity

Nick Hathaway
IG: @nick.hath

Sativa Adams
IG: @sativaadamsart

Jen Aboki
IG: @jenaboki

Kristin Mangam
IG: kat_seeks_19

Allison Leonard
kiss5tigers.blog

Connor Orrico
Twitter: @connororrico

Shawn Coss
IG: @shawncoss

Romane
IG: @bipolarbear_art

Cover Illustration by Dave Combs

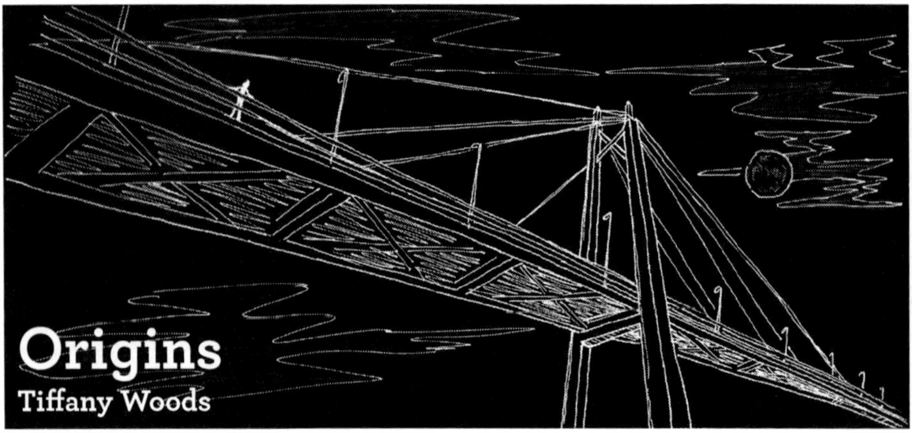

Origins

Tiffany Woods

There is a beginning to my Bipolar Disorder somewhere, although that beginning is debatable as-to whether or not its narrative starts at earliest symptoms - a date which is not clear - or the point of diagnosis. Looking back, it seems there may have been earlier manifestations of Bipolar Disorder in my life than were apparent during my younger years. At the ages of fourteen onward, I was no stranger to seeing two and three o'clock in the morning, completing homework, projects, and practices despite rising at nearly six o'clock the same day. I was a highly productive and efficacious student. My teenaged years were pure joy coupled with nearly relentless energy. If I were to behave the same way today as I did in high school, I would be inarguably manic. However, I managed to retain stability although I was very sleep-deprived at points. Most of my high school days I had coffee in the morning and would not eat or drink anymore until I returned home at the end of the day, sometimes as late as five or six o'clock.

At university I was involved in every extracurricular which pertained to my degree program, and I was successful; trusted to lead; a Dean's List student. In the spring of my freshman year, something strange happened. I didn't prepare for my exams and opted to stayed up late with friends instead of working; I flirted with other guys and broke up with my then boyfriend on a whim; I ate very little. I barely passed my classes that semester due to my poor exam performances despite having stellar grades up to that point. Those few wild days passed and I chalked them up to typical irresponsible collegiate behavior. This now appears to have been my first observable hypomanic episode, although years would pass before this could be identified as-such. Sophomore year was a breeze; I was back on the horse and continued to excel.

Summer of my sophomore year, more strange days came but this time they'd hang on for nearly eight years. I studied abroad and began drinking a lot. While in Western Europe, I recall looking over a bridge on a walk and inwardly noting a lack of desire to live. I thought, "If I died on this trip, that would be okay." Thoughts like these were anathema to my person prior to this moment. When I returned to The States, I recall driving four hours to meet a guy in person I'd only been introduced to online. No one knew where I was going, and it prompted an emergency search on the part of my parents who believed I was with a friend in a different part of the state. I spent the night with a stranger. On the way, I had the thought, "You could die doing this," because I was behaving in a blatantly unsafe way, yet, this did not elicit fear or apprehension from me. My inhibitions were not merely lowered: they were gone. I have always said what makes a person who they are includes what they abstain from. "Who I was" had been replaced by something else entirely.

By the beginning of the fall semester I was sleeping for twelve and fourteen hours daily. I missed classes. I was starving myself and my peers noticed; exercising in largess. At one of my lowest moments, I opened the gun storage my parents owned, stared at the weaponry, and seriously contemplated suicide. Instead, I called a suicide hotline. Pouring all of my newfound dysfunction out verbally seemed to bring me back from the edge. **Many thanks to mental health emergency services.** I felt I had worked myself so stringently over the years, this must be rebound madness: I'd never slacked off before; never slept so much; never engaged in risky behaviors. My body was forcing me into the opposing corner, or so I thought.

My parents brought me to my general practitioner, who prescribed an antidepressant. I cannot stress enough how much worse being on an SSRI (Selective Serotonin Reuptake Inhibitor) made my condition. Years later, I would learn about the damaging affects SSRIs can have on undiagnosed Bipolar patients when they are prescribed in the absence of an antipsychotic or mood stabilizer (Cascade, Reites, Kalali, & Ghaemi, 2007, Antidepressants in Bipolar Disorder). I was having a mixed episode - behaviors meeting the criteria of both a manic and depressive episode. Prior to beginning this medication, I was hanging onto my responsibilities by my fingernails. Three months after, I withdrew from college.

I was having a mixed episode - behaviors meeting the criteria of both a manic and depressive episode.

My professors were shocked and remarked most students who withdraw do not return. It placed my parents, who had been paying for my education, in a precarious financial situation. The time off from school that fall semester helped, but the SSRI I received had to be changed four times before it was obvious this was a class of medication I shouldn't be taking. The studies suggesting Bipolar patients respond poorly to SSRIs alone were new, thus I continued to be treated as a patient with depression by my general practitioner whereas now the poor reaction to SSRIs would be a sign of possible Bipolar Disorder. I needed to see a psychiatrist but was ignorant to my own needs. After all, from my perspective, the primary issues were oversleeping and desires of self-harm. The other erratic behaviors, which were equally disruptive, seemed to me to be choices rather than compulsions. Sadly, I did not report my manic symptoms because I did not know they were symptoms at all.

Spring semester, I reenrolled and appeared to have truly returned. The depression had not left nor had the reckless behaviors, but six months later I had developed unmedicated coping mechanisms which allowed me to achieve laud again. I placed well in vocal competitions, performed decently academically - though it was an intense struggle, I did not fail or withdraw from any more courses - and was elected President of two student organizations. I struggled massively to keep up the pace I'd managed my entire life and couldn't seem to do so with ease. For years I waited for that well-tempered version of myself to return, but she didn't. I struggled with these ups and downs (mostly downs) for years and still believed myself to be clinically depressed because the appetite for death never left.

In the fall of 2013, I received a letter from the adoption agency my parents had used to select me. My biological family was seeking contact with me following my 21st birthday, and I accepted. It was at this time, following the onset of my previously described symptoms, I learned my biological family was riddled with mental illness. For the first time since my strife began, there was a concrete explanation for how this unidentified torment came upon me.

Somehow, I graduated with my Bachelor's. It was time to enter the working world. I struggled to hold down a job. I could seem to work with diligence, even becoming a preferred employee at my workplace, for approximately six months before another crash came in the form of intense depression and anxiety, requiring I resign abruptly. I'd get back up, find another job, and the same thing would happen again. It was exhausting, feeling like such an incredible failure. In that time I married a wonderful man who, knowing my bitter struggles, promised to care for me. Neither of us knew to what extent that promise would be stretched.

Following yet another crash in the early spring of 2018 (six years after my trouble began), I sought out a fifth therapist. I had been in therapy on-and-off the preceding years but never stuck with it because I was in denial about the severity and longevity of the problems I was having. This therapist stuck as I trusted her and believed I really did need help. We spoke about the anxiety I experienced in the workplace and all of my sessions were geared towards getting me back onto my feet as a healthy person who also held down a job. I seemed to be getting better and started to apply for jobs again. Inevitably I was hired, and it was a dream job. I said to myself, surely, if I screw this up, I am incapable of working.

For as tumultuous and sour as the past several years had been, no one knew - least of all me - how much worse it could and would get. Honestly, this is the most difficult chapter of my life to report on for a number of reasons, one of which being I'm still trying to figure out what the hell happened during this period. I started to feel better; confident; capable; energized. The exuberance I had lost in college returned and grew. Everything felt alive - everything within me and around me. The world was beautiful. Ostensibly insignificant events suddenly had profound spiritual meaning. It was as though electricity was flowing through my body. I had boundless energy. Sleep was becoming less and less necessary to fuel the vigor I had for the next day; so, too, was eating. Colors were indisputably different - as-though the saturation had been turned up in my vision. Vibrancy. Ebullience. I was incandescently happy.

All of this energy had to go somewhere. I was over-performing at work and under-performing at home. I was addicted to the lights in city at night; hooked on the coffee shops which stayed open late; reliant upon malls to keep me entertained while I was out alone. When I was home, I would begin one chore and my racing mind would remember another task I needed to complete. Thus, I dropped the chore I had managed to begin and immediately started the next duty. By way of this system, things were often left in more of a mess than when I had first commenced the housekeeping. My mind was on fire. I couldn't keep up - and it felt God-like. I felt God-like. Feelings of confidence turned into feelings of superiority and grandiosity, then invincibility. Of course I could cross a parking lot at eleven o'clock at night alone, unharmed. Why shouldn't I stumble out of a bar in the city alone, drunk, and then get into my car? I was living a life of something other than angst and despondency for the first time in years, and I was making the most of it in the worst way. I was out of control but believed I controlled even the universe. My loved ones, including and especially my husband, scarcely heard from me and rarely knew where I was and when I'd be home. I played music unbearably loudly and could dance to it for two or three hours straight in private. One morning I rose, fire in my veins, and decided I would go for a near four-mile run. I'm not a runner. That is the only run I have ever taken in my life, and it was invigorating. A run like that should have damn-near killed me, but it was as-though my body was on speed, except I wasn't on anything at all. I was amped and ready to party at all hours - up for anything and everything.

It was at this out-of-control point my coworkers began to notice something was off. These hazy feelings replaced the jittery ones. I couldn't focus on tasks at hand or remember what I had been doing or where I was going. The superhu-

I played music unbearably loudly and could dance to it for two or three hours straight in private.

man overachiever they'd come to know suddenly couldn't complete the smallest of tasks. I blamed it on migraines and asked to leave work early a few times. I drove home - an easily forty-five minute drive - in this psychotic state. My self was splitting - I believed the person I was supposed to be at home was me and the person responsible for all of the debauchery was a different person with a different name entirely. This alter of mine was now an afflicting force I had no command over. I couldn't tell reality from dreams. I had difficulty conversing. Talking should take fractions of a second but it took me many, at times, to comprehend what had been spoken to me. I blacked out. Whole days erased from my memory.

There is an expression in the Bipolar community: "what goes up must come down". I remember "waking up" in the shower one day. I refer to this waking up as a mental restimulation of parts of my mind which had gone dark with madness. I called for my husband to leave work. I explained to him I thought I was very, very sick and needed help. We discussed having me psychiatrically hospitalized. In hindsight, that is what needed to happen, but I had a misunderstanding of what psychiatric facilities did. I wasn't one of "those" people; I wasn't crazy. With time I realized if I hadn't gone mad, then where I had I gone? I was one of "those" people, and being one of "those" people wasn't the worst thing one could be.

My therapist had not seen me in months and was, thus, clueless about recent events. What I had to share with her was shocking. She pressed me to answer truthfully whether or not I had taken any recreational drugs. Beyond drinking, the answer was no. I would be asked this question numerous times by different professionals because if I hadn't been taking a stimulatory drug, I had been psychotically manic - there was no in between. I was diagnosed as having Bipolar Disorder Type I with Psychotic Features after nearly eight years of suffering and was, for the first time in my life, medicated.

I went from sleeping two to four hours a night to sleeping nine or more hours; not eating or drinking to doing both heartily; taking no medications to taking four or five at a given time. Though I had crashed, I was still coming down from mania and the drugs I was initially prescribed were harsh. There is a joke in the Bipolar community: you can't be manic if you're sleeping. Those drugs were heavily sedating and I had the best sleep I've ever gotten in my life, but it took a good two or three hours after rising to truly wake up from a mental fog.
As my manic symptoms began to fade the severity of all that had happened while I was manic began to sink in. I had multiple appointments each week between talk therapy, psychiatric visits, and support groups. Many tears were shed during that period. How could my adult life, which had already been so difficult up to this point, have gotten any worse?

I had a lot of existential questions following this episode and it has taken a good year to fully convalesce and find a cocktail of medications which effectively prevent mania and balance depression without overly sedating me. Though I

This is not a letter of bad news: this is a photograph of a great and lengthy struggle I win in the end.

had to leave my previous job - which I enjoyed very much - I've been doing well enough these days to consider working again. Whether or not I'd ever work again had a big "question mark" on it until recent weeks. Now, it seems it is time to dip my toe in the water and see, now that I'm healthy and my Bipolar Disorder is self-managed at home, whether or not I can handle a traditional job or if that tips the delicate balance of my psychological wellbeing.

However the pieces may fall, I have learned some pretty astonishing truths about mental illness I'd never have understood if I hadn't taken ill myself; I've met marvelous and beautiful people on this journey I'd have never met if it weren't for psychotic mania; I've had opportunities to make a difference with my life force I wouldn't have otherwise if Bipolar Disorder had not manifested in me.

This is not a letter of bad news: this is a photograph of a great and lengthy struggle I win in the end. It has been scary and heartbreaking not to have the burden-free life I envisioned for myself, but I see this as a form of growing up. We all have our baggage and this is mine. I'm still learning how to carry it while moving forward.

/'pōəm/ /nəm'bər/ /'kə-sēnō/

by mike vinopal

+ The low white noise din of the $lot ma¢hine$, the windowless chamber-cave of false optimism +
+ & ja¢kpot gold blinking bling, the bizarre caricatures of rambling gambler$ of +
+ northwest corners of Midwestern ruin, steel mills churning pollutant in the distance, +
+ smokers pluming breaths of carcinogens, last breaths of existence, slosh down +
+ cough medicine rendered from the handles, pull down, hope for ri¢he$, +
+ wait for random light to shine upon your good fortune, ATM's +
+ glimmer in the corners, warnings, could be winning$, could be failures +,
+ lost equity, lost self control & compulsory spending, lights flutter +
+ multi-colored blinkings in your thinking, you are sinking while drinking, +
+ sinking quarter$ dollar$ & token$ of hope to lifelines of rope +
+ for the next fix not dope but something intangible & imaginable yes, +
+ but a risk nonetheless probabilities flying possibilities trying +
+ to get the best of your mind count the cards no clocks +
+ no time just signs berating your senses pretenses of defense +
+ of finan¢ial gain, bringing inevitable pain to your brain, +
+ stress & strain. But maybe you win, with that (1)one drop +
+ in the bucket you say, "Fuck it, why not? might get hot! +
+ Got paid($) today wanna roll it over stack it up walk away," but +
+ rarely does it go that way some say it's grace & faith not +
+ luck & fate, but it's just numbers### Keep the beat +
+ feel the count. Be omnipresent of what we +
+ all are holding. Become emboldened by, +
+ the awareness of, your environment +
+ know that you are inside of it +
+ *proceed with caution* & +
+ calculation. Lights +
+ blink, bells ding +
+ wheels spin +
+ deep in a den of sin +
+ the hold sings +
+ with ign of +
+ dollar$$$ +
+ flowing down +
+ word spiral +
+ into the bass +
+ mint to be +
+ c o u n t e d +
+ c o l l e c t e d +
+ appropriated +
+ & projected. +

- (V)V +

Does Bipolar Cause Hallucinations?

Crystal Raypole

The Shift by emjivi

If you know anything about bipolar, you're probably familiar with the most typical, well-known symptoms: severe swings from mania (an extremely elevated mood) to depression (a low mood).

But bipolar is a complex condition that can present in different ways. In fact, four distinct presentations exist: bipolar I, bipolar II, cyclothymia, and bipolar due to another medical or substance use condition.

Some people with bipolar I will never have a depressive episode, while people living with bipolar II don't experience classic manic episodes. Instead, their mood episodes range from mild mania (hypomania) to depression. And if you have cyclothymia, you might not realize you're living with a mental health condition at all—symptoms are often mild enough that they seem like nothing more than moodiness, though others might notice changes in your behavior.

What many people don't know, though, is that bipolar doesn't just involve mood symptoms. It's actually somewhat common to experience psychotic symptoms, generally during an extreme high or low.

Psychosis involves a break with reality. In other words, it becomes difficult to distinguish what's real from what isn't real. But this usually doesn't happen all at once. Instead, the psychotic symptoms can come on gradually, making it even more difficult to understand what's happening.

Psychotic symptoms can vary. At first, you may notice some difficulty understanding others or making yourself understood. You might have trouble concentrating or begin feeling suspicious of other people. It's also common to lose track of time, feel emotionally numb, or become confused about where you are. Psychosis can also manifest as delusions or hallucinations.

What causes them?

Medical experts aren't certain why

some people with bipolar experience hallucinations and other psychotic symptoms. They do know, however, that these symptoms tend to happen when mood episodes are particularly severe. You likely won't experience psychotic symptoms with hypomania, for example, or a mild depressive episode.

Hallucinations can also relate to any delusions you experience. A delusion, or fixed belief in something that isn't true, is another psychotic symptom common with bipolar. Delusions of grandeur, for example, often occur during manic episodes. A grandiose delusion might lead you to believe you have unique or special powers that protect you from harm or make you superior in some way. A related hallucination might involve hearing or seeing people praising your abilities.

You can hallucinate during depressive episodes, too. Depression often involves feelings of pessimism or doubt, and it's not uncommon to have feelings of paranoia, or paranoid delusions, with a depressive episode. You might believe a friend wants to rob you and hallucinate them telling someone else about their plan to take your money once you fall asleep.

It's important to note, however, that delusions don't necessarily trigger hallucinations, or vice versa. While they can seem to reinforce each other, they can also happen independently.

What do hallucinations feel like?

Bipolar hallucinations tend to be auditory. In other words, you're more likely to hear things, such as voices speaking to you, rather than see or feel things that aren't really there.

These hallucinations might involve voices that seem friendly or non-threatening. The voices you hear might converse with you, laugh at your jokes, or offer guidance. But hallucinations aren't always pleasant. You might hear voices that scream or threaten you, encourage you to hurt yourself, or say unkind things.

It's also possible to experience other types of hallucinations, though these are less common.

Olfactory hallucinations involve smells, and tactile hallucinations involve sensations that have no physical cause. Crawling sensations on your skin is one common tactile hallucination. With a visual hallucination, you might see a person, object, or even unusual lights. Visual hallucinations are fairly rare, however, especially with bipolar.

Hallucinations can be mood-congruent, which means they match your mood. For example, you might hear voices that moan, cry, or tell you no one cares about you during a depressive episode.

When they don't match your mood, hallucinations are classified as mood-incongruent. If you hear voices laughing or talking excitedly during a depressed episode, you're having a mood-incongruent auditory hallucination.

In some cases, a mood-incongruent hallucination can make you feel as if some other person or power is trying to control your mood or behavior. This can lead you to do things you might not otherwise do. You might take risks, act impulsively, or attempt to hurt yourself or someone else.

Existing research on mood-incongruent bipolar psychosis suggests these symptoms are often more serious, and you may need in-patient medical support to manage them. So, while you'll want to get professional support for delusions, hallucinations, or any other psychotic symptoms, it's recommended to seek immediate help from a therapist for mood-incongruent symptoms.

How do I know I don't have schizophrenia?

There's some overlap between the symptoms of bipolar and schizophrenia, which sometimes leads to misdiagnosis.

Symptoms that can appear with both conditions include:

- disorganized or confused thoughts
- trouble concentrating or focusing on specific tasks
- substance misuse
- loss of interest in usual activities
- trouble attending to daily needs
- hallucinations
- delusions

Schizophrenia typically involves more severe symptoms and a greater disconnect from reality. So, while bipolar hallucinations typically only happen during an extreme high or low mood state, people living with schizophrenia may have more regular or persistent hallucinations and delusions.

Many people with schizophrenia also have jumbled or incoherent speech and slow or unusual movements. These symptoms can sometimes happen with manic episodes, but it's less common.

To sum up, if you experience occasional hallucinations or other psychotic symptoms that seem to align with mood episodes, bipolar is the most likely cause.

What can I do about them?

Hallucinations can feel unsettling and scary, to say the least. They can also become serious, especially if you hear voices saying negative things or encouraging you to hurt yourself.

While you may not be able to get rid of hallucinations entirely, managing bipolar effectively can often reduce them and help you feel more able to manage them. The tips below can help.

Tell someone you trust

It's a good idea to have a trusted support person you can reach out to when experiencing a hallucination. They can help ground you and keep you safe during the episode. You may not realize you're hallucinating, so it's important to talk to someone if you believe you're hearing voices or seeing things that aren't there.

Develop a routine

Many people living with bipolar find that establishing regular times for exercise, sleep, meals, and socialization helps reduce both the frequency and severity of mood episodes.

As part of your routine, consider avoiding alcohol and making a point of eating nutritious meals. These changes also tend to help relieve bipolar symptoms.

Work with your therapist to find the right treatment

A trained mental health professional can provide a diagnosis and help you explore helpful approaches to treatment.

Many people do need medication to manage bipolar mood swings and psychotic symptoms. If you're already taking medication but don't notice much improvement, mention this to your care provider. A different medication may be more helpful. A therapist can also help you explore strategies to cope with hallucinations and other symptoms you experience.

Mr. Constructed And The Big Idea
Andrew Diaz

A long time ago back in 2006 before I was diagnosed with bipolar disorder type 2, I was severely depressed and sitting in my first apartment with just a table from Ikea and a chair. I sat there and made this drawing "Mr. Constructed And The Big Idea". Years later after being diagnosed I realized how my mind was telling me something was wrong. Mr. Constructed was a character I invented to portray how I really felt. Half of me was the fake persona, a mask I wore so people wouldn't know how depressed I was. The other side of the face portrayed how I really felt inside. Behind Mr. Constructed was what I called "Engineered City", It was the city that represented what was going on in my mind. There is the depressed part of the city with its decayed buildings and the manic side with its abnormal shaped structures.

I look back at this piece and it brings me great sadness and also comfort in knowing all the answers are in me.

Mental Health Analogy
@dorota.chioma.art
A3, inks on paper

I was reflecting on mental health, its invisibility to others, its existence within us.
Most of it is underneath the visible fruits of it.
Like a tree.

Its appearance depends on its roots, the soil it is grounded in, the nutritions it is getting and the external factors of weather, climate, mercy of its cohabitants.

The same with the mental health, it needs to be fed properly and it will grow and look beautiful when all the factors play its part.
It is hard to maintain it in a good shape.
There are factors beyond our control but trees are strong and resilient and although there are seasons when it changes the outlook, there is still beauty in its each appearance.
Sometimes the beauty visible to others is at the high cost of holding on, withstanding storms, healing from wounds inflicted on it by circumstances

and sometimes cruelty of these circumstances knocks down some leaves and even branches ...

@dorota.chioma.art

Rock Steady:
Brilliant Advice from My Bipolar Life

by Ellen Forney

Book Review by Dave Combs

I met Ellen Forney several years ago through working on a project with her cousin Steve. Steve appears in Ellen's graphic novel memoir, *Marbles: Mania, Depression, Michelangelo & Me*, which I had read a few months prior. That was the first time I'd met someone I'd seen as a character in a graphic novel, which was kind of a surreal experience. Ellen is very open about having bipolar disorder, and she and her book *Marbles* played a major role in giving me the courage to share my own story. She even gave me a membership card to "Club Van Gogh" so I also could be a card-carrying crazy person. I had known she was working on a follow-up to *Marbles*, but life got in the way and I didn't get around to reading her more recent 2018 book, *Rock Steady*, until now.

First impression, the book has a graphically bold cover and the velvety smooth, matte laminate finish is pleasant to the eyes and to the touch. The book even comes with cut-out-able placeholders (some people might call bookmarks). It starts off with the dramatic narrative of Ellen being told that she has to go off lithium which has been so helpful in maintaining her stability for fourteen years. Anyone who's ever had to switch from meds that are working knows how frightening it can be. She explains that she needed a guide to stability and had the realization that here she was writing one! She explains early on that though the book is focused on bipolar disorder, anyone can benefit from its advice about seeking balance in order to "Rock Steady".

SMEDMERTS is the acronym for the keys to stability, or the Rock Steady Strategy, seen on the following page. An overview of each of these metaphorical keys is given and sometimes humorously illustrated throughout Chapter One. Like Chapter One, the rest of the book contains a wealth of information from years of lived experience.

Chapter Two details therapy including misdiagnoses. Chapter Three goes into coping tools. Chapter Four is about Insomnia. Chapter Five talks about meds and side effects. Chapter Six explains warning signs and how to deal with them. Chapter Seven is about finding like-minded company, and Chapter Eight reads like an encouraging letter to a good friend. Thanks, Ellen!

One of my favorite aspects of the book is the page of "merit badges" at the end of each chapter. These badges would all make for a great collection of stickers (hint-hint).

I highly recommend this book for anyone who wants to better understand bipolar disorder. Its graphic novel format is very digestible and actually makes the typically dull task of learning about a mood disorder a lot more enjoyable and entertaining. If you enjoyed *Marbles*, you'll love *Rock Steady*!

THE KEY, KEY THINGS TO STAY ON TOP OF ARE:
GET ENOUGH SLEEP,
+ IF MEDS ARE PART OF YOUR TREATMENT,
TAKE YOUR MEDS.
Rx
OTHER KEY THINGS ARE:
EAT WELL,
SEE YOUR DOCTOR + STICK TO YOUR THERAPY,
HAVE A MINDFULNESS * MEDITATION PRACTICE,
EXERCISE REGULARLY,
HAVE A PRETTY REGULAR ROUTINE,
AN ARRAY OF COPING TOOLS,
+ A SOLID SUPPORT SYSTEM.
ellen forney
ROCK STEADY
Brilliant Advice FROM MY Bipolar Life
SMEDMERTS

breathe.

Spiraling by Shades

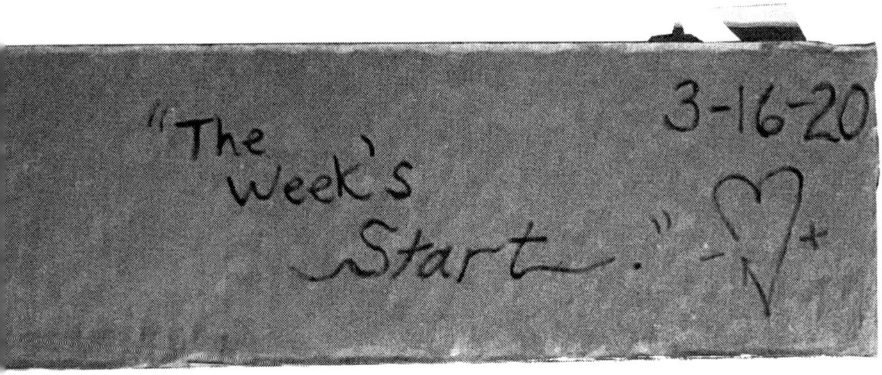

Mike Vinopal

I made this collage "The Week's Start" as a way of celebrating the anniversary of getting out of the hospital a little over six years prior.

It was Pi Day, 2014, couldn't forget it if I tried, as a fixation on numbers is a feature of my mania and it seemed like the hospital staff was fucking with me. So I sort of laughed to myself as I signed the discharge papers to be released into the care of my parents.

There is something very helpful & healing for me to focus on cutting up old print material, upcycling it to create what are often surreal pieces, reminiscent of one of my faves, Salvador Dali. These images from an old CD booklet represented the ego-shattering & rebuilding that has taken place since that important day in my life, my re-birthday. -(V)V+

Bipolar Disorder is Simply Complicated

Ruth River

****Trigger warning – mention of suicidal thoughts****

My official diagnosis of bipolar disorder came 13 years ago. There were plenty of signs before then, I just didn't want to deal with the reality of what that diagnosis would mean. I grew up with a bipolar mother and grandfather who were completely out of control, and I swore that if I was ever diagnosed I would kill myself. At 28 years old, my symptoms couldn't be ignored anymore. I was constantly suicidal, and I was hallucinating "shadow people." So many of the mentally ill people I've spoken to have seen the shadow people that I actually want to believe they are real. Once my diagnosis came, it took quite a bit of counseling to convince me that just because I have bipolar disorder, it doesn't mean that I'm going to be like my mother and grandfather. Just like any individual, each person will have their own unique story with the illness. That is why I will also call on some of the experiences of others who have written about bipolar.

Bipolar Disorder is complex and difficult to define simply. In Sherivan Dijk, MSW's book *The Dialectical Behavior Therapy Skills Workbook for Bipolar Disorder*, she defines bipolar as "a biological illness that causes unusual shifts in your mood, level of energy, and ability to function in different aspects of your life (for example, working or going to school, taking care of yourself, and maintaining relationships). This illness used to be called manic depression, because it was thought that people with the illness would fluctuate only between episodes of highly elevated, euphoric moods, and episodes of major depression. More recently doctors have realized that the illness is not quite that black and white – that there are many moods that actually occur on a spectrum" (Pg. 5). I can relate to every word of this definition. I am not able to work at this time. Also, it would be difficult to count how many relationships I've lost due to bipolar, whether it was because I was manic and too bombastic, or depressed and couldn't manage to return phone calls. Of course, the illness is far more complex than the scope of this simple definition. Dijk describes how this definition has evolved, and more than likely will continue to evolve.

Dijk also lays out some of the symptoms that can occur during depressive and manic phases. Just a few of them will be mentioned here. Depression can include persistent low mood, increased or decreased appetite, difficulties falling asleep, social isolation, and feelings of worthlessness (Pg 7). Mania can include elevated mood, racing thoughts, irritability, feelings of euphoria, and thrill seeking (Pg 9). As you can see, mania has some conflicting symptoms. How can you have an elevated mood, and be irritable at the same time? In my experience, I've had manic episodes that made me feel on top of the world and invincible. I've also had episodes where I was extremely irritable, argumentative, and overwhelmed by the amount of racing thoughts. There is another type of mood alteration called a mixed episode. This is worse than either mania or depression as it includes symptoms of both states. I've found that these episodes are the most dangerous for me. During these times I want to die, and I actually have the energy to make and sometimes even try to carry out a plan. When I'm depressed I don't have the energy to deal with something that ambitious. When I'm manic I can be self-destructive, but it usually comes in the form of spending all my money or drinking too much.

There are two trains of thought when it comes to speaking about the term bipolar disorder. One way of thinking is that you should refer to yourself or others as "having bipolar" and not "being bipolar." The logic behind this is that the person is not their illness. Julie Fast is an author who has bipolar. She subscribes to this train of thought. In her book *Loving Someone with Bipolar Disorder*, she says "When your partner is ill, their beliefs about themselves and the world are often distorted. If you try to talk with them about your relationship, work, or life in general, you often talk to the bipolar disorder instead of the person you love" (Pgs 9-10). She believes that bipolar is an internal enemy that keeps you on guard.

I am bipolar. Of course, that doesn't mean that is all I am. I am also a musician; I have a deep love for cats, and so many other things.

The other train of thought is that the bipolar disorder cannot be separated from the person. It is integral to who they are. This is what I believe. I am bipolar. Of course, that doesn't mean that is all I am. I am also a musician; I have a deep love for cats, and so many other things. I would recommend that whichever of these you believe to be true, just try to be respectful to whatever the person you are talking to believes.

So, what is it like living with bipolar disorder? Kay Redfield Jamison is a psychologist who is bipolar. In her book *An Unquiet Mind*, she says, "For as long as I can remember I was frighteningly, although often wonderfully, beholden to moods. Intensely emotional as a child, mercurial as a young girl, first severely depressed as an adolescent, and then unrelentingly caught up in the cycles of manic-depressive illness by the time I began my professional life, I became, both by necessity and intellectual inclination, a student of moods" (Pgs 4-5). It can be a wild roller coaster ride, joyous at times, and devastating at others. I have made a lot of spontaneous, yet brave decisions in my life that probably would not have happened without bipolar disorder. Some of these decisions worked out, some didn't. Before I was diagnosed and medicated there were times I believed I could accomplish anything if I put my mind to it, and because of this belief I often made it happen. That is the big picture. What is it like day to day? I question everything I think and feel. I question who I really am and so much of my past. How happy is "too" happy and indicates mania? Is my anxiety and depression due to environmental factors, or am I heading towards an episode? Much of the time it's difficult to just let myself be in the moment. However, experiencing this illness has given me a much deeper compassion for what others are going through, and my life probably would have been quite a lot more boring without it. Jamison describes this well. "The vividness that mania infuses into one's experiences of life creates strong, keenly recollected states, much as war must, and love and early memories surely do. Because of this, there is now, for me, a rather bittersweet exchange of a comfortable and settled present existence for a troubled but intensely lived past" (Pg 211). Jamison recognizes that her life would not have been the same without this disorder. I hope to get to a point where I can be as reconciled with my past and present life as she is.

Right now is a time where there are movements to include and celebrate diversity. There are those who strive for inclusion of neuro-diversity as well. People who have bipolar or other mental illnesses do experience life differently from others. Jamison says, "at the end of the day, the individual moments of restlessness, of bleakness, of strong persuasions and maddened enthusiasm, that inform one's life, change the nature and direction of one's work, and give final meaning and color to one's loves and friendships" (Pg 216). Those of us with bipolar disorder don't think like everyone else and don't experience life in the same way as others. I believe adding different perspectives to the world is a marvelous thing.

Stability Illustration and Haiku by Nikki Reed

Everyday struggles
Matching my insides to out
Up. Down. Back and forth

Kansas, Oz

Nick Hathaway

I am The Scarecrow.
A body in patchwork,
skewered by a wooden rod,
roasting on a spit,
sun-stained,
picked at by crows - a daily routine -
head hemorrhaging hay,
in need of a brain.

I am The Tin-Man.
A metallic face,
muzzled by rust,
sickly blue under the glow of a computer monitor,
eyes two bloodshot error messages,
who can't quite reach his oil can - a bottle of pills -
an empty cryogenic chamber,
in need of a heart.

I am The Lion.
A chest-thumping caricature,
self-important,
wiry hair settled into a fierce mane,
a pride's inheritance of ginger hair and green eyes,
echoing an empty roar - a manic roar -
the king of wild eyes,
in need of courage.

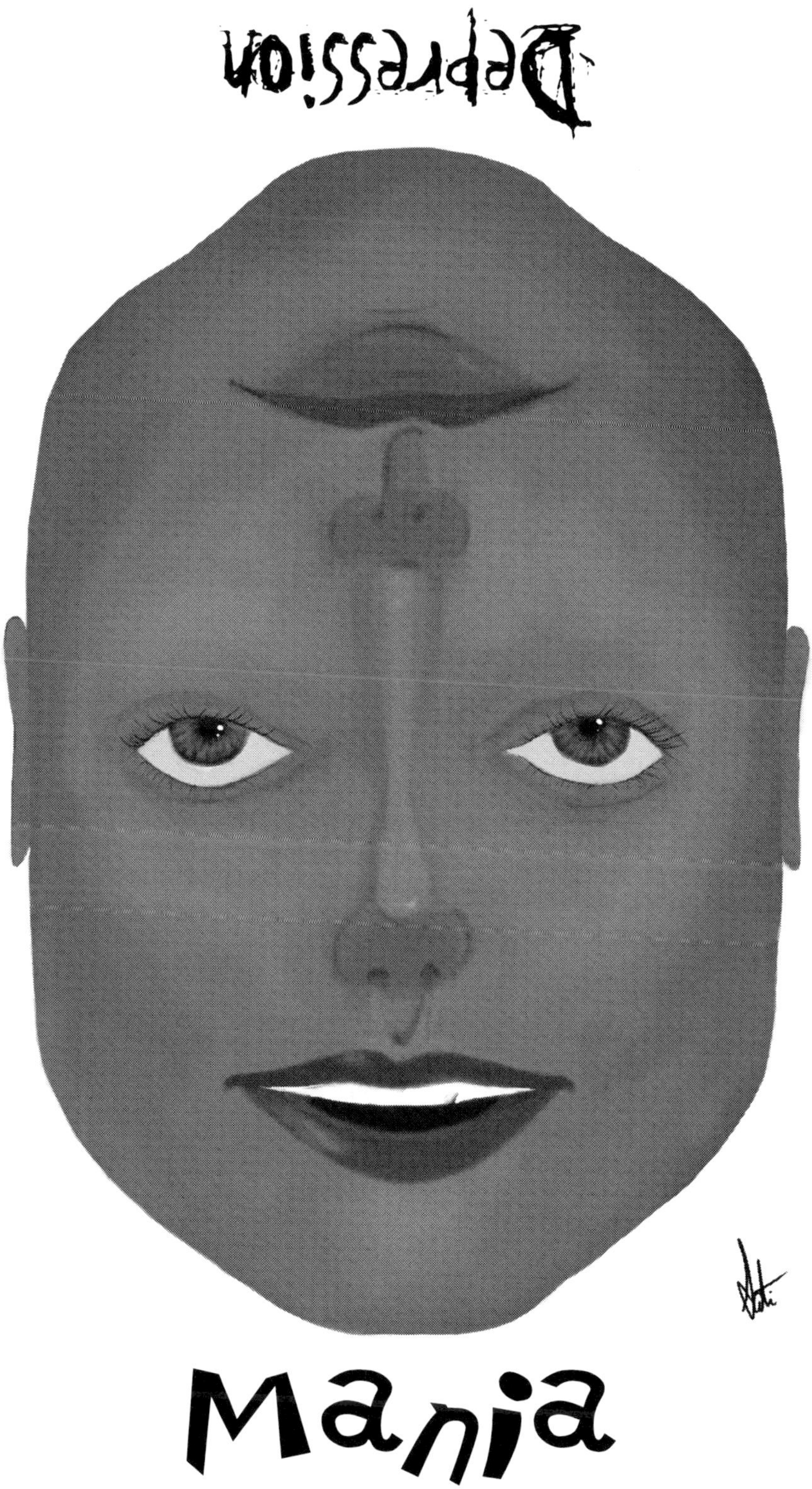
Depression
Mania

Mental Health Artist Series Stickers

Order your mental health artist series stickersheets at thiszinehasissues.com. These 8.5" x 11" stickersheets are full color, vinyl, and removable so they won't damage surfaces. Proceeds from the sales of these stickersheets will benefit the mental health charities of the artists' choice. If you would like to contribute your own artwork to this project visit thiszinehasissues.com/mental-health-stickersheets today for more info about how you can be involved.

Stickersheet by Dave Combs
for Black Mental Health Alliance

Stickersheet by Jen Aboki

I AM NOT YOUR LABELS

A diagnosis of bipolar 1 is one thing, but the labels that go with it are a whole other story. A blend of people's misperceptions, one sided experiences and judgment can lead to a deadly mix.

One thing I have learnt on my journey is that labels can be removed. I like to peel them off slowly, scrunch them in my hand and light them on fire. Strangely, some of these labels are very persistent and keep coming back.

the Eschaton returns
Kristin Mangam
2019, pen and ink, inkjet print

The girl in the artwork, it's a self-portrait made during a manic episode that's become a personal archetype for mania. She's who I see in the mirror and what I feel like when I'm riding that paranoid high.

Not Just a Bipolar Thing

Allison Leonard

I am bipolar. I have been diagnosed with bipolar II. I describe it as all the depression, half the mania.

What do I mean by that? Well, for me, my baseline mood is a kind of mild depression. My depressed times might be every bit as bad as bipolar type I – though my personal depression does not include the psychosis that can plague bipolar I people – but my manias do not get as high. They are called hypomania, where "hypo" means "under". I say, if mania makes you feel ten feet tall and bulletproof, then hypomania makes you feel seven feet tall and good in a street fight. Still unrealistic but not as extreme. The other difference for me, is that I am something of a unicorn. There are all different kinds of unicorns but they have a few traits in common: Everybody has heard of them but nobody has actually seen one. I am a bipolar unicorn. I am that one in a million person whose psychiatrist got the drug cocktail right the first time. Oh, there have been a few tweaks, but the first set of drugs worked and when I try to tweak it, it usually is worse.

Getting diagnosed was a strange thing. I expected to be told I was depressed. I understood depression. I felt it on a daily basis. Not suicidal depression, more like Thoreau's life of quiet desperation. Anhedonia, right, where nothing is enjoyable. The chronic wondering whether there might be more to life, asking again and again, "Is this all there is?" Yeah, depression, surely I had that. But the doctor told me I was bipolar. How could that be? I never had a manic episode. I was never the life of the party or self aggrandizing. I wasn't bipolar. And I told him so.

"Here, try this," he handed me three prescriptions. Fluoxetine, which is generic Prozac, I expected. Aripiprazole (Abilify) he said was for ADD, though it is an atypical antipsychotic which is often prescribed for bipolar as well as for treatment resistant depression. The doctor explained that ADD and bipolar often co-exist. I still wasn't convinced about the bipolar, but perhaps my chronic depression was treatment resistant? Since I wasn't sure what that meant, I thought that could be true. (I have since learned that treatment resistant means treatments have been tried unsuccessfully.) Lamotrigine, aka Lamictal, was the surprise ingredient. It's an anti-convulsant, meaning it stops people from having seizures such as with epilepsy. It turns out bipolar and epilepsy may be related. At the time, I was told the lamotrigine was a mood stabilizer which works on depression. Many mood stabilizers work on calming the mania but lamotrigine works by raising depression. I didn't at the time think, "Oh, this man is treating me for bipolar," I just thought I must have a bad depression because it took so much medication.

Then I went shopping.

I enjoy shopping. I like buying stuff, it makes me happy. One day shortly after seeing the doctor, I woke up and wanted to go shopping. I took the bus to the old Prestonwood Mall, which had been converted into big box stores. I started at Wal-Mart, went to an arts and crafts store, a clothing store, an office supply store, a pet store, a dollar store, a cosmetics store, a shoe store, and ended up at Barnes & Noble. I bought close to $100 worth of books and magazines, but I had purchased something in every store I entered. I called my daughter to come get me. I bought her a fancy-pants coffee and some pastry as a thank you. And when I went to the doctor, I told him he was right about the bipolar. I didn't get manic, but I sure did become untrustworthy with money. He just smiled.

I have learned that my hypomania generally involves spending money, especially money I can't spare. I have also figured out that I do become a little full of myself. I can recognize that feeling when it comes on so that I can almost stop it by will power. I thought it was PMS but it turns out to be part of bipolar. I also remembered deciding at one point in my life that big emotion was not good for me. I tried to keep an even keel as much as possible. Being bipolar meant that rather than big emotion throwing off my equilibrium, in fact, the reverse was true. I lost my inner balance and it resulted in me being very expressive with my emotions. Too expressive, sometimes. Sleep also became a way to measure my bipolar. I have been pulling all-nighters since 3rd grade. Turns out those were probably hypomanic episodes. Not that kids that young are supposed to be bipolar, but I don't believe there are no early signs.

We did make two changes to my medicine. One was early in the process. I was so slowed down by the drugs that I couldn't hold a conversation. Friends worried about me. I told the doctor and he cut me back on the aripiprazole. Later, I went to my aunt's funeral and I couldn't cry. She took me in when I moved to Texas and I loved her so much.

I am a complete person with my good points and my bad points. Some of them are related to being bipolar and some are not.

I wanted to cry, to be sad about losing her. That would be normal. When I saw the doctor again, I told him about it. He adjusted the lamotrigine. I feel like extreme highs and lows might be a sign of bipolar, but everybody has good days and bad days. It's average to have up days and down days, and in some ways, I hope to be average.

Bipolar is not just a diagnosis. It does have some distinct features that I navigate on a regular basis however it is not the only label you could give me. I am also short, middle aged, gray haired, a mother, an only child, a Scorpio, and on and on. These are aspects of me that make me who I am, but they are not the sum total of me. So it is with being bipolar. It affects my whole life, but it's not all that I am.

I am a complete person with my good points and my bad points. Some of them are related to being bipolar and some are not. I had a roommate say to me one time, "I'm sure it's one of your bipolar traits, but sometimes you can be a little oblivious to my hints about what I need you to do." Well, it's true I'm oblivious to hinting, but it has to do with my family of origin, not my bipolar. I am more than my diagnosis. It's not a bipolar thing, it's an Allison thing.

a frail mind

Connor Orrico

heartbeat mocking,
breathing doubting,
powerless words
a potent weight,
full pockets of stones
dragged wave after wave
into wearied sea to free
my bipolar-fatigued brain.

BIPOLAR DISORDER I
@SHAWNCOSS

The Turtle and the Hailstorm: A Bipolar Love Story

Holly Combs

The first part of this article is an excerpt from an interview written for Erin Huber's Mother Artist Project in 2014. You can read the full interview at: http://themotherartistproject.blogspot.com/2014/03/holly-apeel.html

When I met and married my husband Dave, I thought that would be freedom. He was this amazing, challenging man—(now twenty) years later, he still is. But I married him under false pretenses. I thought he was a moody, quirky artist. A rebel, complete with leather jacket and unpredictable actions. And all of that was kind of true, but all of it was kind of a sickness. That's the trick of mental illness, or any long-term illness, I expect. It's a part of you. Sometimes it makes you more you than ever—more of the worst of you. Sometimes it means more of the best. I carried my husband on my back for years thinking I was alone in the struggle. Wondering why he couldn't see how the weight of him was slowly killing me. But it wasn't his fault. He didn't know. No one knew. Undiagnosed. Saddest word ever. So in those years there were a lot of highs and lows. The lows were knock-you-down-in-a-ditch-at-the-bottom-of-a-cliff low. The funny thing was that the highs were just as terrifying. I was always sitting on the edge of my seat, waiting to jump . . . or be pushed. But somewhere in the exhilarating, frightening mess, we made art together—and two beautiful children. And I started to grow. I'm not gonna lie. I didn't do it well. Sometimes I took root in the wrong places. There were side trips down the road of adultery for both of us. It wasn't just not pretty—it was scarring. I can show you them, if you ask. But we grew. He grew into an understanding of who he was and how to get control of the illness that too many times brought him to death's door, with him willingly opening it to peek inside. And I realized that being unique didn't mean I had to do it all on my own. We leaned. On God. On family. On friends. On each other. I thank God every day that my kids were too young to remember much about those years. But I also thank God every day that I do remember. And that maybe I can give them some of the wisdom and beauty that came out of the struggle. It's remembering that gives me the strength and confidence to teach others now. Because I have scars, I can see the hurt in others more easily. And I don't just let it go. Not anymore. Secrets are so overrated. I always say, "Your stories are not given to you to keep, they are given to you to share so that others don't feel alone."

"Your stories are not given to you to keep, they are given to you to share so that others don't feel alone."

– Holly Combs

I wrote the above words six years ago, and there are some additional other things I've reflected on since then.

• **People with bipolar often find people who have therapeutic skills to be in relationship with.** At first, this may seem like a good pairing. It's not. It took many years (15+) for me to realize that I should not be Dave's therapist. Don't be your bipolar loved one's therapist or educator. The person you will neglect is yourself, and you'll be wasting your physical and emotional energy. It will likely only make things even worse.

• **Set boundaries (requires the most energy and discipline).** It's the most important aspect of all of this.

• **Mental illness is isolating both for the person who has it and for the person who loves them.** Because of stigma, I didn't want anyone to see it. The pain of loneliness was suffocating.

• **Get your own therapist (which I didn't do until about a year and a half ago) and don't lean too heavily on friends.** They are probably uneducated and will say dumb shit. It's much too heavy of a burden to put on anyone other than a professional. So don't be a therapist for others or ask that of anyone other than a professional you pay. If the therapist you find doesn't work, keep looking. You will know when it is a good match. If you don't have insurance, you can look for a therapist who works on a sliding scale. That's what I did, and it changed my whole life. (I love you, Laura. Thank you!)

• **Mental illness is a monster.** It is abusive, unkind, and thoughtless to both the person it dwells within or takes possession of, as well as those around them. In short, FUCK MENTAL ILLNESS.

• **Commit to become educated.** This will allow you to be more efficient and not dig a deeper hole or allow yourself to silently sink deeper into the quicksand. Knowledge is power, and you will need to be very strong to walk this out. I believe in you. The payout is worth it.

• **Be able to separate the person from the illness.** Identify the two parts of the person and speak to the part that is relevant to the situation. Don't direct your feelings toward the human in front of you. For example, I say, "Baby, I understand that your illness is talking right now, and it's hurting my feelings, but I know that's not you. Let's pause until we can communicate in a healthier way with each other." (See above – set boundaries) Bipolar has no ability to reason or speak soundly and logically.

• **Never use someone's mental illness against them in an argument.** That's pretty self explanatory.

• **Deal with your codependency issues.** Not dealing with them leads to no longer being able to identify the line between yourself and that other person. The sickness draws you in like a moth to a flame and you will certainly get burned.

• **You are not your loved one's caretaker.** If you aren't inspiring them to take care of themselves, then you aren't taking care of you. Do not, under any circumstances, carry that person. You'll lose your own ability to walk.

• **Remember that you can have a working, loving, balanced relationship with a bipolar person.** Both people must be committed all these things I've said above in order for this to work.

• **Neglecting my need for support, therapy, self-care, and making myself a priority has created lifelong damage.** PTSD, anxiety, panic attacks, and depression are all things I now face as a direct result of the stigma of not talking about mental illness. I am no longer a victim of the imposed social stigmas of mental illness and I will bravely move forward in the knowledge that vulnerability is sexy. It makes me remember that I have to get up every day and remind myself that **I am enough, I am beautiful, I am strong, and I am worthy**.

This Zine Has... a Blog

Just can't get enough of *This Zine Has Issues*? Follow along online at *thiszinehasissues.com/blog/*

To read (almost) daily personal posts about the ups and downs of living life with bipolar I disorder from *This Zine Has Issues*' editor, Dave Combs, click the link "This Dave Has Issues" or to filter out personal posts and read only the posts related directly to *TZHI*, click the "uncategorized" filter. The blog is intended to be a behind-the-scenes look at *This Zine* and there is often additional up-to-date information not found in the printed issues about how you can be a part of making it all happen. If anything you read on the blog resonates with you, please share the posts on Facebook or Twitter with the provided buttons in each post.

If you would like to be a guest blogger, have an idea for a post about mental health, or if you just want to say hello, email *thiszinehasissues@gmail.com*.

Paper plane thoughts
Romane (@bipolarbear_art)

For me, this drawing represents the feeling of being overwhelmed by my thoughts. Each paper plane represents a thought pointing at me. The quantity of paper planes illustrates the level of intensity of my experience with all kinds of thoughts. The thoughts can be positive, negative, intrusive, etc.

RESOURCE GUIDE

Need Immediate Help In An Emergency? Call 911

If you or a loved one is in immediate danger calling **911 and talking with police** may be necessary. It is important to notify the operator that it is a psychiatric emergency and **ask for police officers trained in crisis intervention** or trained to assist people experiencing a **psychiatric emergency**.

NATIONAL SUICIDE PREVENTION LIFELINE™ 1-800-273-TALK (8255) suicidepreventionlifeline.org

National Suicide Prevention Lifeline
1-800-273-8255
suicidepreventionlifeline.org

The National Suicide Prevention Lifeline connects you with a crisis center in the Lifeline network closest to your location. Your call will be answered by a trained crisis worker who will listen empathetically and without judgment. The crisis worker will work to ensure that you feel safe and help identify options and information about mental health services in your area. Your call is confidential and free.

CRISIS TEXT LINE |

Crisis Text Line

Text HOME to 741741 from anywhere in the United States, anytime, about any type of crisis.

Crisis Text Line is free, 24/7 support for those in crisis. Text 741741 from anywhere in the US to text with a trained Crisis Counselor. Crisis Text Line trains volunteers to support people in crisis. With over 100 million messages processed to date, we're growing quickly, but so is the need.

National Domestic Violence Hotline
1-800-799-SAFE (7233)

Trained expert advocates are available 24/7 to provide confidential support to anyone experiencing domestic violence or seeking resources and information. Help is available in Spanish and other languages.

National Sexual Assault Hotline
1-800-656-HOPE (4673)

Connect with a trained staff member from a sexual assault service provider in your area that offers access to a range of free services. Crisis chat support is available at Online Hotline. Free help, 24/7.

NAMI HelpLine
1-800-950-NAMI (6264) or info@nami.org

The NAMI HelpLine can be reached Monday through Friday, 10 am–6 pm, ET.

The NAMI HelpLine is a free, nationwide peer-support service providing information, resource referrals and support to people living with a mental health conditions, their family members and caregivers, mental health providers and the public. HelpLine staff and volunteers are experienced, well-trained and able to provide guidance